AMAZON PARROTS
TS-115

Overleaf and Pages 158-159: Blue-fronted Amazons playing on toy ladders.Most Amazon parrots love to climb; therefore, a wooden, Amazon-sized ladder, available at your local pet shop, will probably become one of your pet's favorite toys.

Photographs: Toni Angermayer, Glen S. Axelrod, Dr. Herbert R. Axelrod, Cliff Bickford, Theodore Brosset, Tom Caravaglia, W. de Grahl, Isabelle Francais, Earl Grossman, Anders Hansson, Fred Harris, Dr. Irwin Huff, Ralph Kaehler, H.V. Lacey, Gary Lilienthal, Don Mathews, Max Mills, Dr. E.J. Mulawka, Horst Mueller, K.T. Nemuras, Stefan Norberg, Linda Rubin, Vince Serbin, Louise van der Meid, Vogelpark Walsrode, Dr. M.M. Vriends.

Art: R.A. Vowles.

Originally published in German by Franckh'sche Verlagshandlung, W. Keller & Co., under the title *Unsere Amazone: Anschaffung, Pflege, Richtig füttern, Freundschaft schliessen.* First edition ©1986 by Franckh'sche Verlagshandlung, W. Keller & Co.

Distributed in the UNITED STATES by T.F.H. Publications, Inc., One T.F.H. Plaza, Neptune City, NJ 07753; in CANADA to the Pet Trade by H & L Pet Supplies Inc., 27 Kingston Crescent, Kitchener, Ontario N2B 2T6; Rolf C. Hagen Ltd., 3225 Sartelon Street, Montreal 382 Quebec; in CANADA to the Book Trade by Macmillan of Canada (A Division of Canada Publishing Corporation), 164 Commander Boulevard, Agincourt, Ontario M1S 3C7; in ENGLAND by T.F.H. Publications Limited, Cliveden House/Priors Way/Bray, Maidenhead, Berkshire SL6 2HP, England; in AUSTRALIA AND THE SOUTH PACIFIC by T.F.H. (Australia) Pty. Ltd., Box 149, Brookvale 2100 N.S.W., Australia; in NEW ZEALAND by Ross Haines & Son, Ltd., 18 Monmouth Street, Grey Lynn, Auckland 2, New Zealand; in SINGAPORE AND MALAYSIA by MPH Distributors (S) Pte., Ltd., 601 Sims Drive, #03/07/21, Singapore 1438; in the PHILIPPINES by Bio-Research, 5 Lippay Street, San Lorenzo Village, Makati Rizal; in SOUTH AFRICA by Multipet Pty. Ltd., 30 Turners Avenue, Durban 4001. Published by T.F.H. Publications, Inc. Manufactured in the United States of America by T.F.H. Publications, Inc.

Amazon Parrots

Red-lored Amazons
(Amazona autumnalis)

HELMUT PINTER
TRANSLATED BY WILLIAM CHARLTON

Contents

Facing: A seven-year-old Yellow-crowned Amazon (Amazona ochrocephala belizensis).

Species

A pair of Yellow-billed Amazons (Amazona collaria).

Amazon Parrots

Christopher Columbus brought the first amazon parrots back to Europe from his first voyage to the New World. The species in question was the Cuban Amazon Parrot (*Amazona leucocephala*), which at that time apparently was also abundant in the Bahamas. These parrots were the first animals Columbus and his sailors encountered in the New World. A full half century later, the Swiss naturalist Conrad Gesner (1516–1565)

Facing: *The Cuban Amazon* (Amazona leucocephala) *was the first Amazon species brought to Europe.*

Lilac-crowned Amazons (Amazona finschi). *Note the differences in color between individual Amazons of the same species.*

described this bird extremely accurately in his two-volume bird book, *Historia animalium,* which was originally written in Latin and published in 1557. The book was translated into German during the same year. Among the birds described, the "Papagay" that "is white on top of the head" and in which "a bright cinnabar color is conspicuous on the lower part of the neck but particularly on its wings" takes its proper place. Today the Cuban Amazon Parrot is a great rarity, and one would be fortunate to see it even in a zoo or bird park.

The name amazon parrot, or amazon for short, is of considerably more recent origin. This name was first used by Dr. Karl Russ, who published a number of popular books on birds as house pets in the 1870s and 1880s. Prior to this, these primarily green colored parrots were simply called green parrots or short-winged parrots.

The genus Amazona, which is the scientific name of our amazon parrots, comprises a total of 27 species, but some of these species have to be ruled out as house pets. According to the CITES Treaty—which, after all, has also been obligatory for the Federal Republic of Germany since 1977—any capturing of the species listed below is prohibited. The trade in birds that are included in the following list and those that were already in Europe before this treaty took effect is subject to the control of conservation authorities.

Cuban Amazon Parrot *(Amazona leucocephala)*

Puerto Rican Amazon Parrot *(Amazona vittata)*

Red-crowned Amazon Parrot *(Amazona dufresniana rhodocorytha)*

Red-spectacled Amazon Parrot *(Amazona pretrei)*

Vinaceous Amazon Parrot *(Amazona vinacea)*

Yellow-shouldered Amazon Parrot *(Amazona barbadensis)*

Red-tailed Amazon Parrot *(Amazona brasiliensis)*

St. Vincent Amazon Parrot *(Amazona guildingii)*

Headstudy of a Yellow-billed Amazon (Amazona collaria).

St. Lucia Amazon Parrot *(Amazona versicolor)*

Imperial Amazon Parrot *(Amazona imperalis)*

Red-necked Amazon Parrot *(Amazona arausiaca)*

Because these species cannot be kept as house pets, they will not be discussed further in the text.

In the following pages we wish to consider in somewhat greater detail the amazon parrot species that are obtainable on the market today. The majority of them belong to three species. Because two of these species are divided into several

subspecies (races), which also have distinct names, the number of species appears to be greater to the layman than it actually is.

Orange-winged Amazon Parrot
Amazona amazonica

This is one of the most frequently encountered species. Its range extends across all of northern South America east of the Andes; that is, over large parts of Brazil, Surinam, Guiana, Guyana, and eastern Venezuela, as well as the parts of Colombia, Peru, Bolivia, and Ecuador that lie east of the Andes.

The length is as much as 33 centimeters. The ground color is green, often with a grayish green tinge on the underparts. The front parts of the cheeks are yellow, the rear parts green. On the crown above the bill is a yellow patch, which in some individuals extends over the forehead to the base of the upper mandible. Others may exhibit a fairly small yellow patch on the crown and have a blue gray or bluish violet forehead. The lores and the area around the eyes are bluish violet, and in some specimens the yellow color of the front of the cheeks extends below the lower

mandible. In general, the color distribution of the head markings can be quite variable. It is not unusual to find a pure yellow feather on the extreme outside of the carpal edge. The secondaries have dark bluish violet tips. The tail feathers are green and are more or less yellowish on the underside; the outermost feathers have red inner vanes. The orbital eye ring is grayish blue, and the iris is orange. The bill is yellow-gray horn colored and darker toward the tip. The feet are pale gray to grayish brown. Corresponding to their very large range, Orange-winged Amazon Parrots are extremely variable. This is particularly true of the head coloration, the color of the tail feathers, as well as the color of the bill and feet.

Orange-winged Amazon Parrots make very good house pets. As a rule, they become tame quickly and some develop into tolerable talkers. They are among the most frequently imported species and are usually obtainable on the market. They have also been bred repeatedly in captivity.

Blue-fronted Amazon Parrot
Amazona aestiva

This species, which is highly

Orange-winged Amazons (Amazona amazonica) *are among the most commonly encountered Amazons, and they are often available for sale in pet shops. They tame rather quickly and may become good talkers.*

prized as a house pet, has two recognized subspecies (races). The range of the first subspecies—the nominate form *(Amazona aestiva aestiva)*—extends over southeastern Brazil, approximately from Pernambuco in the north to a latitude of 30 degrees in the south. The bend of the wing of this species is red, and it is therefore also known as the

The Blue-fronted Amazon (Amazona aestiva) *is a popular house pet, although it may be a bit more timid than Amazons of other species.*

Red-shouldered Amazon Parrot. The second subspecies *(Amazona aestiva xanthopteryx)* occurs farther to the west, in the interior of the country. Its range directly adjoins that of the nominate form. This subspecies has yellow on the bend of the wing, and is therefore also called the Yellow-winged Amazon Parrot. It should be noted, however, that Blue-fronted Amazon Parrots are quite variable in coloration, and that a smooth gradation in coloration occurs between the two subspecies.

The length is as much as 37 centimeters. The ground color is green; the feather edges have dark borders. The forehead is blue. The crown is yellow, but in some specimens the front part of the crown is also blue, whereas in others there is only a suggestion of blue on the forehead. The area around the eye is yellow. The speculum is red. The secondaries have violet tips. The tail feathers are green with yellowish tips and red bases. The outermost tail feathers have blue edges. The orbital ring is white to grayish blue. The iris is orange. The bill is dark gray, almost black in some specimens. The feet are gray.

Blue-fronted Amazon Parrots make outstanding house pets. They can become very tame and devoted, and some of them show good mimicking ability. They have been successfully bred many times.

Yellow-fronted Amazon Parrot
Amazona ochrocephala ochrocephala
This amazon parrot occurs in Venezuela, Surinam, Guiana, Guyana, eastern Colombia, and northern Brazil.

The length is as much as 37 centimeters. The ground color is green, darker on the back and lighter on the

The Yellow-fronted Amazon (Amazona ochrocephala ochrocephala) is among the most popular Amazon parrots.

Tail feathers from a Yellow-fronted Amazon (Amazona ochrocephala ochrocephala). These were taken from the same bird, from the same position, during different molts; note the difference in coloration.

underside. The forehead and crown are yellow. A narrow stripe of green feathers extends between the yellow crown and the light gray orbital ring. The speculum and bend of the wing are red. A few yellow feathers are usually present on the carpal edge. The tail feathers are green with lighter tips. The outer tail feathers have red inner vanes at the base. In some specimens the lower part of the thighs is more or less yellow. The iris is orange. The bill is dark gray, lighter at the base, and the lower rear portion of the upper mandible is often reddish. The feet are blue-gray to gray.

Second to the Orange-winged, as the most commonly imported amazon parrot, it is well-suited as a house pet.

Panama Amazon Parrot
Amazona ochrocephala panamensis

This is a subspecies of the

Panama Amazon Parrots (Amazona ochrocephala panamensis). These birds are members of a subspecies of the Yellow-fronted Amazon. Panamas are usually smaller than the Yellow-fronts.

17

Yellow-fronted Amazon Parrot. Its range encompasses eastern Colombia and western Panama. Very similar to the Yellow-fronted Amazon Parrot, but usually somewhat smaller.

The maximum length is 32 centimeters. In this subspecies the yellow of the crown is separated from the orbital ring by a distinct blue green stripe. The bend of the

Blue-fronted Amazon (Amazona aestiva).

wing usually lacks red or yellow feathers. The most obvious difference between this subspecies and the Yellow-fronted Amazon Parrot is the color of the feet, which are grayish white in the Panama Amazon Parrot with nearly white nails.

Panama Amazon Parrots are considered to be good mimics and are well-suited as house pets. They too have often been successfully bred.

Yellow-naped Amazon Parrot

Amazona ochrocephala auropalliata
This is also subspecies of the Yellow-fronted Amazon Parrot. In the wild it occurs in Nicaragua, El Salvador, Guatemala, and southern Mexico. It has a characteristic appearance and can scarcely be mistaken for any other amazon parrot. This is a large, thick set amazon parrot, which can reach a length of 39 centimeters. The color is a saturated green. Some specimens exhibit a blue green luster. There is a large yellow spot on the nape. The plumage is otherwise a uniform green. The bill is dark gray and lighter toward the base. The orbital ring is gray, and the iris is orange. The feet are light gray. Some individuals of this subspecies

have nearly white claws as well.

Yellow-naped Amazon Parrots are teachable and for the most part exhibit a very good mimicking ability. Unfortunately, these talented talkers are seldom imported. Nevertheless, they have been successfully bred.

Double Yellow-headed Amazon Parrot
Amazona ochrocephala oratrix

The common name of this subspecies came about in the following way. In previous decades, the Yellow-shouldered Amazon Parrot *(Amazona barbadensis)*, which is protected today, was often imported, and usually was known in the trade by the name Lesser Yellow-headed Amazon Parrot. To prevent any chance of confusion, this species became known as

The Double Yellow-headed Amazon (Amazona ochrocephala oratrix) is yet another subspecies of the Yellow-fronted Amazon. This is the largest of the A. ochrocephala Amazons and is one of the largest of all Amazons.

the Double Yellow-headed Amazon Parrot. This amazon parrot is the largest subspecies of *Amazona ochrocephala* and one of the largest amazon parrots of all.

The length can reach 41 centimeters. It occurs in Mexico and Honduras. In fully colored specimens, the head and neck are yellow, and in many specimens the lower part of the thigh is also yellow. The bend of the wing is red, usually with a few yellow feathers on the carpal edge. The bill is a whiteish yellow horn color. The orbital ring is white to yellowish white. The iris is red and is often lighter in the forward

The Green-cheeked Amazon (Amazona viridigenalis) is considered a bit too screechy to be a popular house pet.

Amazon Parrots are well-suited as house pets, although they are usually livelier and often louder than their smaller relatives. Individuals are frequently good mimics, and they have often bred in captivity.

The following amazon parrots are occasionally offered on the market, but they are imported considerably less often, and are usually sold at higher prices.

Green-cheeked Amazon Parrot
Amazona viridigenalis
This species occurs in northeastern Mexico. It attains a length of 33 centimeters. The ground color is green with the underside being lighter. The forehead and crown are red and the occiput is bluish. The cheeks are an intense grass green. The bill is yellowish horn colored. The orbital ring is white and the iris is yellow. The feet are light gray to green gray.

Green-cheeked Amazon Parrots are not as well-suited as house pets because they are very lively, often very loud, and can screech shrilly. Once acclimated, however, they can become very devoted. They are better suited to keeping in aviaries and have bred in captivity.

half. The feet are light gray to light brown. Infrequently, one also finds somewhat variably colored individuals of this amazon parrot; for example, birds with isolated yellow feathers in the plumage. Their green feathering is clearly lighter on the underside, and the nape feathers exhibit dark edging. Youngsters are uniformly green at first, and the yellow head feathers appear only gradually.

Double Yellow-headed

Green-cheeked Amazons are much better suited to aviary keeping than to being kept as single pets.

Above: *This bird is one of the Mealy Amazon subspecies,* Amazona farinosa inornata.

Mealy Amazon Parrot
Amazona farinosa
This species is found from southern Mexico through Central America and South America to the Mato Grosso in Brazil. Several subspecies of this amazon parrot occur. The length can reach 38 centimeters. The ground color is dark green, with the underside being lighter. The crown is yellow, yellow red, or yellow with interspersed small red feathers. Depending on the subspecies, other crown colors like green or blue can also occur. The nape feathers exhibit dark edging. A characteristic of all Mealy Amazon Parrots is that plumage looks as if it were dusted with flour (hence the name). The orbital eye ring is gray, and the iris is red. The

Below: *A member of the nominate subspecies of Mealy Amazons,* Amazona farinosa.

bill and feet are gray.

Mealy Amazon Parrots are rarely imported. Because they generally become tame quickly and are good mimics, they are well-suited as house pets. They are quiet in temperament, although if frightened or bored, they can screech appallingly. They are decidedly good natured toward other birds, and are well-suited for keeping with other parrots.

Festive Amazon Parrot
Amazona festiva
Two subspecies with disjunct ranges occur. The nominate form, *Amazona festiva festiva,* lives in the upper Amazon region and the second subspecies, *Amazona festiva bodini,* is found in the Orinoco river basin in Venezuela. The principal distinguishing feature between these subspecies is the red color of the loral band in *Amazona festiva bodini,* which extends as far as the forehead and crown.

The length is 34 centimeters. The ground color is a weak yellow-tinged green. The nape feathers exhibit dark edging. A reddish brown stripe runs from eye to eye across the forehead. A narrow zone above and behind the eyes and the throat are bluish. The typical characteristic, which safely

Festive Amazon (Amazona festiva). This species is a popular captive bird, but today they are imported with less and less frequency.

distinguishes them from all other amazon parrots, is the bright red plumage on the back and rump. This red marking is not present in youngsters. The bill and feet are gray. The orbital ring is blue-gray and the iris is orange.

Festive Amazon Parrots are extraordinarily amiable birds, and scarcely another amazon

parrot is as easily tamed. Nevertheless, today they are offered very sporadically on the market. No successful breedings are known.

White-fronted Amazon Parrot
Amazona albifrons
This amazon parrot is found in western Mexico and Costa Rica. With a length of 26 centimeters, it is one of the smallest amazon parrots. The ground color is green. The forehead is white, merging with blue toward the crown.

White-fronted Amazons (Amazona albifrons), *especially those birds which are raised by hand, are becoming more and more popular as housepets.*

In youngsters the crown is yellowish. The area surrounding the eyes is red, with the orbital ring white, and the iris yellow. With the White-fronted Amazon Parrot one can distinguish the sexes of adult birds with certainty by their color. In the male, the front of the wing coverts of the primaries is red, whereas these red feathers are lacking in the female. The tail feathers are green with yellow tips. The bill is yellow horn colored. The legs are light gray.

White-fronted Amazon Parrots have been imported more often in recent years. If one can obtain a youngster, this amazon parrot will certainly become an amiable house pet and can develop a very good mimicking ability. Older, wild-caught birds, on the other hand, only become tame by way of exception and can be terrible screechers.

Red-lored Amazon Parrot
Amazona autumnalis

This species has several subspecies. Most of the birds that have been offered on the market so far have been of the nominate form, *Amazona autumnalis autumnalis,* which occurs in eastern Mexico and northeastern Nicaragua. The length is 34 centimeters. The ground color is green, with the underside slightly tinged with yellow green. The forehead and front of the crown are red. The rear part of the crown and the nape are blue lilac. The nape feathers exhibit black edging. The upper part of the cheek is bright yellow. The speculum is red. The upper mandible is grayish white, darker on the tip and the lower margin.The lower mandible is gray.

Like the Green-cheeked and the White-fronted amazon parrots, Red-lored Amazon Parrots do well as house pets if young birds can be obtained. Older birds become acclimated only with difficulty and screech loudly and penetratingly. They are better suited for keeping in an aviary.

The Red-lored Amazon (Amazona autumnalis) *has several subspecies, but the most commonly seen is the nominate form,* Amazona autumnalis autumnalis.

Artist's rendering of some Amazon Parrot heads

Blue-fronted Amazon
(Amazona aestiva)

Double Yellow-headed Amazon
(Amazona ochrocephala oratrix)

Yellow-naped Amazon
(Amazona ochrocephala auropalliata)

Yellow-fronted Amazon
(Amazona ochrocephala)

Panama Amazon
(Amazona ochrocephala panamensis)

Imperial Amazon
(Amazona imperialis)

St. Vincent Amazon
(Amazona guildingii)

Yellow-lored Amazon
(Amazona ochrocephala xantholora)

Black-billed Amazon
(Amazona agilis)

Green-cheeked Amazon
(Amazona viridigenalis)

Lilac-crowned Amazon
(Amazona finschi)

Blue-crowned Amazon
(Amazona farinosa guatemalae)

Festive Amazon
(Amazona festiva)

Cuban Amazon
(Amazona leucocephala)

White-fronted Amazon
(Amazona albifrons)

Mealy Amazon
(Amazona farinosa)

27

The Black-billed Amazon (Amazona agilis), and the Hispaniolan Amazon (Amazona ventralis), are rarely seen in captivity.

Other species of amazon parrots may also be offered on the market, but this is rare. Such species as the Lilac-crowned Amazon Parrot (Amazona finschi), Black-billed Amazon Parrot (Amazona agilis), Yellow-billed Amazon Parrot (Amazona collaria), or Hispaniolan Amazon Parrot (Amazona ventralis) should not, however, be acquired as house pets. As far as possible, these extremely rare species should be kept for breeding only. In no case should such rare and expensive birds be purchased as "status symbols."

Facing: The Lilac-crowned Amazon (Amazona finschi) is not often kept as a pet, but those who have had them say they are friendly and playful.

This pair of Red-lored Amazons (Amazona autumnalis) *are well acquainted and enjoy each other's company.*

Things to consider before purchasing an amazon parrot

Any acquisition of a house pet should be thoroughly thought over, and this is particularly true of the purchase of an amazon parrot. One should guard against "buying on impulse." An important question that one should ask and answer before an acquisition is: Do I have enough time for a single bird? Amazon parrots are by nature extremely gregarious birds, which are encountered either in flocks or in pairs in the wild. If one keeps an amazon parrot alone as a house pet, then the people in its environment must take the

Facing: *A Black-billed Amazon* (Amazona agilis).

A pair of Yellow-faced Amazons (Amazona xanthops). *Note the alert, cheerful expressions.*

the parrot or does not have the necessary time for the animal, then the amazon parrot can easily develop vices such as screeching or feather plucking. If one cannot make the necessary time, but still desires to keep an amazon parrot, then there is only one solution: one keeps two birds. Yet the second bird does not necessarily have to be an amazon parrot. Most amazon parrots also get along well together with a small cockatoo or a Grey Parrot. Which birds are compatible in this case must be determined by trial and error. Ask your animal dealer. Maybe "your" bird has already found a playmate in the store. It can, of course, also turn out that two particular birds will be totally incompatible, which could also certainly happen with two amazon parrots.

Five rules for buying an amazon parrot follow.

Rule I: Only keep a single bird if you have a lot of time to devote to it.

Rule II: Never buy an amazon parrot with the firm expectation that it will become a good talker. It is true that many amazon parrots have a considerable mimicking ability, but this does not necessarily have to relate to human speech. In practice, it can very well be

place of others of its kind, and a few hours in the evening are simply not enough for this. An amazon parrot that must spend the whole day confined to a small cage is a very unfortunate and unhappy bird. Amazon parrots are equipped with one of the best developed brains of all birds. If one does not spend enough time with

the case that all kinds of noises including squeaking doors, dripping faucets, and barking dogs will be more readily imitated than the words that were repeated to the amazon parrot for weeks on end.

Rule III: Do not expect a purchased amazon parrot to act civilized in your home! Amazon parrots—like all parrots—are very messy eaters and scatter food remains all around. Therefore, count on not only needing extra time for regularly cleaning the cage, but also expect to spend additional time on general house cleaning after the arrival of an amazon parrot.

Rule IV: Do not expect the newly acquired amazon parrot to become tame immediately. "Tameness" is a process of establishing trust that takes time.

Tucuman Amazons (Amazona tucumana). *A pair of Amazons should be acquired if one has only a few hours a day to spend with his pets.*

The Green-cheeked Amazon
(Amazona viridigenalis) *is sometimes
called the Mexican Redhead.*

Rule V: Consider that amazon parrots, like all large parrots, can live to a very old age. If properly cared for, an amazon parrot has a life expectancy of at least thirty years, and many of them live considerably longer. Because youngsters are generally imported, the acquisition of an amazon parrot is a purchase for life (and thus the earlier warning against buying on impulse).

What must I pay attention to when buying an amazon parrot?

Before one decides on the purchase of a particular amazon parrot in the pet shop, one should closely observe the particular bird on several occasions and if possible, at different times of the day. While doing so, keep in mind that virtually all amazon parrots on the market are wild-caught birds, which at first can still be quite timid and shy. One should not buy an amazon parrot that is alway quiet or even makes an apathetic impression, irrespective of the time of day.

On the trip to Europe and also in quarantine, the birds are often packed close together. For this reason the plumage of new imports often looks somewhat "disheveled" when they arrive on the market. If no bare (that is, featherless) spots are present in the plumage, this is not serious. Birds that are

Facing: *This pair of Yellow-lored Amazons* (Amazona xantholora) *will keep each other occupied and out of trouble—we hope!*

*Yellow-shouldered Amazon
(Amazona barbadendis barbadendis)
in an outdoor aviary.*

plumage of parrots is continuously "powdered." The powder is supplied by powder down distributed throughout the plumage. The powder down constantly releases a grayish white powder, which makes the plumage water-repellent. For this reason, amazon parrots often look somewhat dusty, particularly if they have not been able to "shower" for a long time.

Make sure that the bird does not sneeze, that the nostrils are open and are not encrusted with deposits, and that its breathing is regular. The plumage in the vent area must not be soiled or matted. Soiled plumage in the vent area indicates diarrhea. The normal droppings of an amazon parrot are compactly formed, moist, and of a greenish white color. If an amazon parrot is disturbed, however, it can release quite watery droppings. This is often the case if an amazon parrot that is not tame is taken from the cage or caught in some other way.

Also inspect the candidate's feet before the purchase. Amazon parrots have a typical climbing foot with four powerful toes. Of these, the two outer toes point backward and the two middle ones point forward. When examining the feet, one

partially bare on the belly, throat, or wings should not be bought, because they could be feather pluckers.

In order to make their plumage water-repellent, most birds treat their feathers with a fat-like substance from the preen gland. With amazon parrots, and with parrots in general, the preen gland is greatly reduced and restricted in its function. The

should make sure that the toes and claws are whole. The horn shield on the toes and legs must be smooth. Healthy parrots perch on one foot while sleeping. However, if they "dose" completely relaxed, which they do quite often in the middle of the day, they may also perch on both feet.

With the bill, one should make sure that the margins of the upper and lower mandible lie uniformly on each other and that the bill, when examined from the front, is straight and not crooked or distorted. The tip of the upper mandible should not be overly long. Bill deformities are very rare with imported amazon parrots; however they can occur. The cause of bill malformations is usually a lack of provision for gnawing

A slouching Red-lored Amazon (Amazona autumnalis). When shopping for an Amazon, always look for a bird that stands upright on its perch.

The White-fronted Amazon (Amazona albifrons) *is one of the smallest and lightest Amazon species.*

brought about by improper keeping in cages. Owing to an unusual joint, all parrots can move their upper mandible independently of the lower mandible, which looks especially funny when they yawn.

Judging the general condition of the body is a problem when buying, particularly for the novice. Whether "our" bird exhibits a normal weight or if it is exceptionally scrawny cannot be determined because of the feathering. The simplest solution is to weigh the parrot. The cage is weighed with and without the amazon parrot. The smallest amazon parrots, such as the White-fronted Amazon Parrot *(Amazona albifrons),* weigh between 200 and 250 grams; Orange-winged Amazon Parrots *(Amazona amazonica)* weigh 320 to 370 grams; Yellow-fronted Amazon Parrots *(Amazona ochrocephala ochrocephala)* weigh 340 to 420 grams; and Blue-fronted Amazon Parrots *(Amazona aestiva)* weigh 400 to 500 grams, with very large individuals up to 550 grams. The largest species, such as the Double Yellow-fronted Amazon Parrot *(Amazona ochrocephala oratrix)* and the Mealy Amazon Parrot *(Amazona farinosa),* tip the scales at 650 to 850 grams. Of course, weight alone does not tell much about the state of health, but a weight control is an easy-to-use method to protect against the acquisition of an emaciated bird. Let us briefly summarize the important points to consider one more time:

— Never buy an amazon parrot that makes an apathetic impression!

— Never buy an animal that sneezes, has gummed up or clogged nostrils, and exhibits

The Mealy Amazon (Amazona farinosa) is one of the largest of all Amazon species. One should never purchase a bird which is underweight for its species.

Blue-fronted Amazon (Amazona aestiva xanthopteryx). *Note the healthy-looking plumage.*

irregular breathing.

— The amazon parrot you choose should have clear eyes. The rims of the eyes must be clean and must not exhibit any scabby deposits.

— The bill should be straight and uniformly shaped.

— Smooth, clean feet with complete toes and claws are a matter of course.

— The plumage in the vent area must be clean.

— A healthy amazon parrot has compactly formed droppings of a greenish white color.

— Bare spots must not be present in the plumage of amazon parrots. Somewhat disheveled and dusty looking plumage is of no significance.

— If one has doubts about the general body condition, one should check the weight.

At this point some readers will certainly want to know: are any amazon parrots that were bred in captivity on the market? This is a legitimate question, because in the species descriptions, we have read that many amazon parrot species have already been successfully bred. Although the number of amazon parrots bred in Europe has increased, particularly in the last decade, the number of these birds is still very small compared to the demand. Birds bred in Europe are therefore rarely ever offered in pet shops. From time to time, however, one can find advertisements by breeders in magazines that deal with birds or house pet keeping.

Red-crowned Amazons (Amazona dufresniana); this species is also called Blue-cheeked. A pair of Amazons will keep each other from boredom and may prevent such bad habits as excessive shrieking and feather plucking.

Red-lored Amazon (Amazona autumnalis salvini) *on a natural wood perch.*

The new home
The proper parrot cage
Sturdy wire cages, with either a bottom drawer or a removable bottom section of metal or hard plastic, are generally used as accommodations for amazon parrots. If the drawer or bottom section is removed, the cage should be open on the bottom, so that one can put it directly over an amazon parrot sitting on the floor. This makes it easier to capture birds, particularly those that are not yet completely tame. The parrot cages common in the trade, with a size of 40 by 40 by 60 centimeters or 50 by 50 by 60 centimeters, are, however, too small for permanent housing. It would be inhumane cruelty to constantly confine such an intelligent and lively creature as an amazon parrot to such a small cage. As soon as the newly acquired amazon parrot has become acclimated, it must be permitted to leave its cage at least occasionally. Only in this way can the development of vices such as screeching and feather plucking be prevented and serious psychological disturbances be counteracted.

So that your amazon parrot has the necessary "room to move about," even in a fairly small cage, it is best to install a climbing stand made up of several perches fastened

Facing: *Blue-fronted Amazon* (Amazona aestiva) *demonstrating that Amazons love to climb, whether from perch to perch or up a ladder.*

Yellow-fronted Amazons (Amazona ochrocephala) *on a typical Amazon Parrot cage. Yellow-fronts are also called Yellow-crowns.*

together crosswise on the cage. The perches should be thick enough that the bird's foot can only reach about two-thirds the way around them. If the perches are too small, the claws are not used enough, and overly long claws are often the result. Conical perches that gradually increase in diameter from 1.5 to 5 centimeters are also well suited, since these take the place of branches of varying sizes in the wild. They offer the amazon parrot a variety of footholds and therefore provide for uniform use of the leg muscles.

Large wire cages as well as small indoor aviaries that can be dismantled are available as standard models. Most pet shops do not have larger cages of this kind in stock, but they can be delivered on short notice. Wire cages can also be built to one's own specifications. Some pet shops also accept orders for wire fronts with doors and openings for food bowls. Fronts of this kind are used with box cages. Box cages are well-suited for keeping parrots, particularly for breeding. If you have some mechanical skill, you can also build the box yourself. Keep in mind that box cages for parrots must be lined with precisely cut Resopal sheets. The exposed front edges are protected against the parrots' bills by means of a metal rim, over which is placed the removable wire front. The box cage should also have a

Amazons should be provided with perches or branches of varying widths so they can wear down their claws.

bottom drawer of galvanized sheet metal.

Make sure that your cage doors have secure locks. I admit this seems logical, but is often not so easy in practice, because large parrots are often expert at opening all sorts of locks. In many cases, only a small padlock helps!

Some parrot cages have an added grating over the bottom drawer, which prevents the bird from reaching the floor. A grating of this kind is sensible only if the floor is covered with newspaper, because the

grating prevents the bird from tearing and scattering the paper. Amazon parrots, however, require sand and grit for digestion. If a grating and newspaper are used, the amazon parrot must have access to sand or fine grit elsewhere. The most practical solution, however, is simply to remove any bottom grating and to spread sand on the floor of the cage.

All of the perches in the cage must be thick enough that the amazon parrot's foot cannot reach all the way around them. The tips of the claws of a perching bird should touch against the wood of the perch and not overlap. This ensures that the

Quite an assortment of Amazons. Left to right: a Red-lored, two Orange-winged, a Blue-front, and a Mealy. Note the difference in sizes between species.

tips of the claws will wear evenly, and prevents excessive claw growth. Conical perches also work well in parrot cages; they allow the bird to choose the thickness it wants while perching.

Most amazon parrots will gnaw and nibble at their perches. This gnawing is important for the normal wearing of their bills, and one should therefore let them

Blue-fronted Amazons in a wrought iron parrot cage. Be sure the cage allows
enough room for ample movement.

Be sure to purchase food dishes of a proper size. This Hispaniolan Amazon (Amazona ventralis) *has dishes which are large enough for him to play in, which makes for too much wasted food.*

have their way and replace badly chewed perches according to need. It would be totally wrong to replace wooden perches with other materials such as metal or polystyrene.

Equipping the cage with four large, sturdy ceramic or stainless steel food bowls has proved to be practical. In the long run, plastic or polystyrene bowls do not stand up to the parrots' gnawing talents. All food and water bowls should be easy to remove from outside the cage. Standard stainless steel bowls, which can be installed on climbing stands or climbing trees, are available on the market.

Where should the complete accommodations be located? So that your amazon parrot will not only like its accommodations but the location as well, a few suggestions: cages open on all sides should stand or hang with at least one side directly on a wall. Even better is a location in a corner of the room. The "backing"

An Amazon should be provided with furnishings which will keep it active and interested. This Yellow-naped Amazon (Amazona ochrocephala auropalliata) is enjoying his particular set-up.

provided by the solid wall will namely have a calming effect on nervous birds and often offers better protection against draft. However, because amazon parrots will

An example of varying widths in wooden perches.

nibble on the wallpaper in such an arrangement, the wall behind the cage must be protected. This is most easily done by means of Resopal panels. "Resopal" melamine resin sheets are mainly used as for exterior surfaces of kitchen cabinets and the like, and are available in many colors and patterns in building supply stores.

It is best to have a suitable sheet cut to the correct size at the store at the time of purchase.

A final comment on cages: never keep an amazon parrot in a round cage. Parrots that have been kept for long periods in round cages frequently exhibit serious behavioral disturbances.

Climbing trees and stands

A climbing stand or climbing tree is appropriate for completing the furnishing of the cage. If little space is available, a few additional perches can be fastened on top of the cage. A large climbing stand or tree should be placed next to the cage so that the amazon parrot can climb directly over to it from the cage. Suitable for climbing trees are gnarled branches of deciduous trees; oak, beech, ash, or maple are recommended woods. Pine leaders, which often withstand the gnawing of amazon parrots for a surprisingly long time, are also well-suited. A

Facing: *Festive Amazons* (Amazona festiva), *and all Amazons, love to perch and gnaw on natural tree stumps and branches.*

Be sure that branches given to the birds have not been treated with chemicals of any kind.

exclusively on the climbing stand or tree. Of course, food and water bowls must also be installed on the climbing tree. In any case, a cage should always be available so that the bird can be confined overnight or if it must be left alone.

Amazon parrots often like climbing in a vertical direction as well. This need can be met by means of a 2—3 centimeter diameter rope or a length of thick chain that can be hung from the roof of the cage or from the climbing tree. If a rope is used, both ends must be secured with hose clamps so that the amazon parrot cannot get tangled in any loose strands.

In the past, amazon parrots were often kept chained by one foot on a stand. Keeping them in this manner is plain animal cruelty. Chaining can, however, be sensible for specific purposes; for example, if one wishes to take an amazon parrot outdoors whose wings have not been clipped. It can also be practical if amazon parrots kept at liberty must be left alone temporarily. Nevertheless, a parrot should only be chained for a short period of time. A parrot is chained by means of a special foot ring attached to a light metal chain.

tree stand can be used as a base for a fairly small climbing tree; the base of a beach umbrella can be used with larger trees. A piece of sheet metal, shaped like an upside-down funnel, attached to the tree will prevent the parrot from leaving the climbing tree. Once properly acclimated, the amazon parrot can generally be kept

The Aviary

Amazon parrots can, of course, be kept in indoor aviaries and in outdoor aviaries during the warmer months of the year. In these aviaries, the parrot can indulge in its natural impulse for movement without escaping or causing damage

Aviaries should provide ample room for movement for each bird and adequate protection from the elements. There must also be enough perches for all birds housed in the aviary.

in the house. Aviary keeping is particularly recommended for breeding attempts.

In indoor aviaries, any electrical lines and outlets must be protected. Electrical lines should be run through metal conduits, and outlets should be protected by wire guards. Normal electrical insulating material will not stand up to the bills of amazon parrots. All aviaries should have at least one solid wall, because solid side walls offer the birds a certain feeling of safety. In a house, the best place for an aviary is a protected corner of a room. In the event that you wish to build such an aviary yourself, the home construction market offers complete wire-mesh frames with or without doors.

Outdoor aviaries must be at least partly roofed over, so that the birds are protected against draft, rain, heat, and cold. Because rats and mice as well as other vermin are attracted by the parrots' food, it is best to build the outdoor aviary on a concrete slab or foundation, which should extend at least one meter into the ground. All weight-bearing metal parts of the aviary structure must be of rust-proof galvanized material (for example, galvanized water pipes or rectangular pipe). For enclosing the aviary, spot-welded wire mesh with a wire gauge of 1.5 to 2 millimeters and a mesh size of 20 to 25 millimeters should be used. Under no circumstances should plastic-coated wire mesh be used, because this will be bitten through by the amazon parrots. The door opening should be large enough that one can comfortably enter the aviary. Don't forget, the door lock should be "parrot-proof."

Facing: *All Amazons thrive on cleanliness; therefore, one must keep their housing as sanitary as possible to prevent the infestation of vermin and the spread of infectious diseases.*

Feeding

Cuban Amazons (Amazona leucocephala) *in the wild include grapefruit among the foods they would naturally eat.*

drinking water for decades does not mean that they were properly fed. It merely shows that they are undemanding and easily satisfied birds. Naturally, it is impossible to offer amazon parrots living in captivity the same assortment of food available in the wild. We can, however, make an effort to feed them a

This Cuban Amazon (Amazona leucocephala caymanensis) *seems to be a very well fed specimen.*

What to feed amazon parrots?

Amazon parrots in the wild have a very wide range of food to choose from, and they principally feed on various seeds and fruits. In addition, they also eat animal food, at least from time to time. Accordingly, the fact that amazon parrots in captivity have survived on an unvaried seed diet and

Amazon parrots enjoy a wide variety of foods in their natural habitats. Owners of captive Amazons should strive to give their pets a healthy diet containing a variety of nutritious foods.

Feeding

Yellow-fronted Amazon (Amazona ochrocephala) *enjoying a drink of water. Amazons should have access to clean water at all times of the day.*

balanced assortment of nutriments.

An examination of an amazon parrot's digestive organs, a well-developed crop a proventriculus, and a ventriculus, shows that they are above all "seed eaters." The digestive organs are complemented by the amazon parrot's bill, which, in combination with the powerful tongue, represents a perfect instrument for

shelling seeds and cracking nuts. In the wild, the various seeds are eaten green and half-ripe as well as ripe. Ripe seeds are also welcomed in the soaked or sprouted state. Besides seeds and nuts, wild parrots also feed on the most diverse kinds of fruits and berries. In addition, they also eat greens of all kinds, tree buds, and even the bark of certain trees.

For this reason we should use nature as a model, if we wish to offer the amazon parrot a complete diet. A mixture of seeds is a dietary staple, of which a good fifty percent should consist of sunflower seeds and the remainder of hulled oats, wheat, and millet. The color of the sunflower seeds is of no consequence; there is no difference in the nutritive value of white, striped, and black sunflower seeds. Sunflower seeds belong to the so-called oil seeds, and their kernels can contain up to 54 percent raw fat. All oil seeds and nuts are sensitive to storage, and even under

Facing: *In the wild, Amazons extract much of their water intake from leaves and the like.*

This White-fronted Amazon (Amazona albifrons) *is enjoying the bark from this tree. Natural wood helps provide minerals needed for the Amazons' health.*

the best storage conditions the kernels can become rancid after a certain amount of time. Rancid oil seeds and nuts are dangerous for the birds. Therefore, every parrot owner should make it a habit to chew a few sunflower seeds from any newly purchased batch of seed. One will be able to taste any rancid seeds immediately.

In addition to this basic food, peanuts (in the shell) and cembra-pine nuts can also be offered. Other nuts, such as hazelnuts, walnuts, and Brazil nuts, must be cracked. Beechnuts and pumpkin seeds are also readily eaten by most amazon parrots.

As soon as we are able to bring back half-ripe seeds from a walk in the country, we should offer the amazon parrot half-ripe heads of wheat and barley as well as

Facing: *Seeds and nuts are popular with all Amazons, which is evident from this Blue-fronted* (Amazona aestiva) *Amazon's expression.*

Amazons will sometimes drink straight from a bottle. Yellow-fronted Amazon (Amazona ochrocephala ochrocephala).

esteemed if they are still soft. Ask a farmer in your area whether he will part with a small amount! Green peas as well are usually well liked. All seeds, peas, beans, and lentils can be fed in sprouted form as a change of pace. The feeding of sprouted seed is especially recommended in breeding. Be careful when sprouting seed; always provide for the necessary hygiene, because soaked or sprouted seed spoils rapidly. To sprout seed, one places normal seeds in a small bowl with water, so that they are

panicles of oats. Kernels of maize, which one offers in the form of whole ears, are highly

Double Yellow-headed Amazon (Amazona ochrocephala oratrix) and *Red-lored Amazon* (Amazona autumnalis autumnalis). *Birds should be provided with mineral blocks, which will provide important trace minerals.*

Blue-fronted Amazon (Amazona aestiva) *occupied with chewing. Chewing helps wear away the bill, which will overgrow if not exercised regularly.*

Black-billed Amazon (Amazona agilis).

bird to bird. Some individuals will eat almost anything, while others take only certain fruits. And don't forget: amazon parrots also eat with their eyes. A colorful mixture stimulates the appetite (and the play instinct)! In my experience, apples, pears, bananas, and carrots are eaten by virtually all amazon parrots.

Besides various berries, some amazon parrots also like to eat rosehips and leaf buds of fruit trees and willows. They like to peel the bark from fruit tree and willow branches, which, however, would seem to have more to do with occupational therapy and bill use than food intake. Of course, only fruit tree branches from trees that have not been sprayed with insecticide may be used.

For some time, complete pellets, which are made specifically for parrots, have been available on the market. According to the manufacturer, these are supposed to be able to completely replace seeds in the diet. This claim could be correct from a physiological standpoint, but the pellets in no way satisfy the fundamental requirements of parrots, because the eating of seeds and nuts is not merely food intake for parrots, but moreover an

covered by about a finger's breadth of liquid. They are rinsed well with water after 24 hours and stored in a covered container for an additional 24 to 48 hours. Mold must not be allowed to form, however, and uneaten sprouted seed should be removed from the cage as soon as possible.

One can offer amazon parrots any sort of fruit and vegetable available on the market. What will and will not be eaten can vary from

Amazons will readily eat bread, but it should not be given too often.

important activity for them, which cannot be replaced by eating a uniform pellet food. Because these food pellets have a very high protein content, they could, however, be of some value as a supplementary food during breeding. Based on my own experience, the same result can be achieved through the supplementary feeding of good-quality dry dog food, which has virtually the same composition as the parrot pellets, but is considerably cheaper.

An important question comes up if an amazon parrot is kept in the house: what can I give my bird from the dinner

A Blue-fronted Amazon (Amazona aestiva) *enjoying some fruit. Fruit is a commodity which is good for parrots once in a while.*

table? With the exception of heavily salted and seasoned foods, and as long as only "bird portions" are given, the answer is almost anything. But this kind of feeding must not be overdone. An amazon parrot can safely gnaw a pork chop bone or chicken leg, or eat a piece of potato, a small piece of cake, or a slice of bread and butter. A bit of the breakfast egg or a piece of roll dunked in milk also suits

Red-necked Amazon (Amazona arausiaca), *one of the rarer Amazon breeds.*

it very well. Over the years, a number of amazon parrots that principally ate from the dinner table have been shown to me, and, in spite of advanced age, were found to be in the best of condition. Perhaps not necessarily because they ate from the dinner table, but quite certainly despite doing this.

Some caution is advised with the feeding of cheese, which most amazon parrots eat avidly. For reasons that as yet have not been clearly explained, after eating too much cheese, casein can accumulate in the crop of some amazon parrots, which causes digestive disorders. For this reason, cheese should be given only quite sparingly; two to three one-centimeter cubes of cheese a week are enough.

Another question that must be answered is: do amazon parrots need animal protein? Apparently, they do not need it for mere existence, but it does appear to be of significance for the production of reproductive cells and for the breeding drive. Amazon parrots in the wild definitely eat insects, at least occasionally, and apparently also worms. I have observed amazon parrots kept in outdoor aviaries eating nestling mice. Nevertheless, whether one

should feed parrots meat during breeding attempts is disputed even among experts. I personally avoid feeding raw meat, which some amazon parrots eat without hesitation, for hygienic reasons. In practice, one can get by just as well with cooked meat, cooked eggs, and a good dried dog food as a food supplement. It is important that foodstuffs of this kind are fed as a planned supplement during breeding and never as the principal food.

That all animals, in addition to nutrients, also need vitamins and trace elements would seem to be general knowledge. How does this apply to amazon parrots? If they are fed as previously described, they should scarcely become ill from a vitamin deficiency, and their requirement for essential trace elements is also ensured with a varied diet. It is important, however, that amazon parrots always have access to a mineral block and coarse-grained sand. Mineral blocks are available in pet shops. Sand and grit are eaten in small quantities by amazon parrots, and support the digestive activity that takes place in the ventriculus.

Drinking water can be given as it comes from the faucet. Make sure that your amazon

Yellow-fronted Amazons (Amazona ochrocephala belizensis). *Note the variations in the head markings.*

parrot always has fresh, clean water at its disposal. The contents of the water bowl should be replaced at least once a day and, if soiled by food remains, droppings, or other dirt, the water must be changed as occasion demands. It goes without saying that the water and food bowls must always be rinsed clean and dried.

A Yellow-fronted Amazon (Amazona ochrocephala ochrocephala) *being stick-trained.*

The first days at home

It is best to bring the new "family member" home in a covered cage. So that the bird does not catch cold on the trip, wrap the cage carefully in a cloth. As soon as you have placed your newly acquired amazon parrot in its future environment, give it time to become familiar with its immediate vicinity. Always move slowly and carefully when approaching the cage to feed or change the water. This is particularly important with amazon parrots that are still nervous or even frightened. If, on the other hand, you have acquired an amazon parrot that has been in a pet shop for a fairly long time, or which was even purchased from private hands, then the first stage of acclimatization can be dispensed with. A bird of this kind can be let out of its cage the next day. With birds that are not yet acclimated, as a rule one must wait two to four weeks before this step. If an amazon parrot is in full possession of its flying powers, let it out of the cage for the first time in the evening under artificial lighting. If you let it out during daylight, the amazon parrot, when it suddenly no longer finds itself surrounded by bars, could use the opportunity to try to fly. Not infrequently, the nearest window will be much the worse for wear than the parrot. Luckily, they amazon parrots are generally hardheaded, whereas normal window glass often will not stand up to the impact of an amazon parrot. For this

Facing: *Yellow-naped Amazon* (Amazona ochrocephala auropalliata). *This bird is obviously hand-tame.*

White-fronted Amazon (Amazona albifrons). *This species is sometimes called the Spectacled Amazon.*

moments. Subsequently, with feet pointing inward and a slightly raised tail, it will no doubt purposefully head for the object that seems to be the best suited for climbing. Amazon parrots do not like to sit on level ground. Only when it feels completely secure in its environment will your amazon parrot voluntarily fly to the floor.

An Amazon should never be let loose in a room unless it is well supervised.

reason as well, wing clipping is recommended at least during the acclimatization period. Later amazon parrots learn to recognize the boundry presented by transparent windowpanes, and no longer fly into them.

If your amazon parrot's wings have been correctly clipped, it will flutter abruptly to the floor a few meters from where it took off. After landing, it will probably sit there slightly scared for a few

Perching on the hand

If one knows that the ground is scary for an amazon parrot because it cannot see very far, one can use this situation for taming. Wait until the amazon parrot again lands on the floor. If it makes no attempt to fly, simply sit down on the floor near it. As soon as it takes its first steps, hold a long stick of suitable thickness (for example, a broom handle) a few centimeters above the floor in front of its feet so that it is forced to climb up on it. If it does not climb up voluntarily, then the stick should be moved gradually toward the amazon parrot so that it sees no alternative but to climb on the stick or to press sideward past the stick. After a few unsuccessful attempts, the amazon parrot almost always climbs on the stick. With a little patience, the bird will soon climb on the stick without hesitation and also remain perched there. The next step is to decrease the distance between you and the bird. To do this, hold the stick a little closer to the bird at every opportunity, or draw it

A Yellow-naped Amazon (Amazona ochrocephala auropalliata) *in the process of being hand-tamed.*

through the hand holding the stick with the free hand when the amazon parrot is already perched on it. In this manner the bird will finally perch right next to the hand on a short section of stick. From there it is only a "small step" from the stick to the hand. To be sure, this training program does not always run quite this smoothly. Be patient and adjust yourself to the tempo "two steps forward and one step back." If you are too impatient, the amazon parrot may try to avoid your hand

Wing-clipping is desirable for a bird who is not yet tame and must adjust to the stress of a new home.

Facing: A hand-tame Tucuman Amazon (Amazona tucumana). When handling your Amazon, it is best not to wear gloves, as gloves will generally frighten the bird.

It is a good idea to keep the Amazon on some sort of chain when taking it outdoors. Too much freedom can be dangerous!

and fly away, or, what is more serious, try to bite the hand that is uncomfortably close. If it manages to bite, then it will usually not end without "bloodshed." One must not, however, make the mistake of putting on gloves as a precaution. Virtually all imported large parrots have a great fear of gloves, because gloves are used during quarantine, routine treatments, banding, and so forth, and amazon parrots have excellent memories. If an amazon parrot attempts to escape or even bite, one should view this as a sign that one has moved too fast. Only patience will bring success, and since every amazon parrot has its own personality, the acclimatization phase can also take varying amounts of time.

Once an amazon parrot has become so used to being close to people that it goes on the hand without difficulty, other attempts at getting closer will be considerably easier. If you wish to hold and stroke your amazon parrot, this is usually easier to do on the head or the breast than on the back or the rear of the body. An attempt at "head scratching" is therefore the most promising at first. How far and how quickly one will get with further attempts to get close to the bird cannot be stated in more detail; you will have to find this out for yourself with "your" bird. All it takes is a lot of patience and understanding. It is also usually true that one family member can do whatever he wants with the amazon parrot, and others can't get to first base! Amazon parrots

Amazons, when at liberty, will usually fly to the highest possible place.

Blue-fronted Amazons (Amazona aestiva).

added that it is extremely rare for parrots to bite out of viciousness; on the contrary, they bite out of fear. Should one happen to get bitten badly enough that a skin injury or bleeding results, the wound should be disinfected before applying a bandage or dressing. This is a basic rule with animal bites, even if the injury appears to be minor.

The amazon parrot and other pets

How does an amazon parrot act if other pets such as a dog or a cat live in your house? One seldom encounters difficulties with dogs, and I know of amazon parrots that are best friends with dogs. In the first place, amazon parrots often can earn a surprising amount of respect from dogs, and, in the second place, a properly raised dog will hardly attack another pet. If a young dog tries to do this to an amazon parrot, it will learn a lesson it will never forget. In my experience, properly trained hunting dogs do not attack pets either. The reason for

often become attached to a particular person. For this reason it can happen that another person, whom the amazon parrot knows just as well, is susceptible to being bitten if he attempts to do "exactly the same thing." For this reason, small children, in particular, should be kept away from an amazon parrot that is not yet fully acclimated. It should be

Facing: *Before introducing new people to the Amazon, it must be fully acclimated to its new surroundings and owner.*

78

Blue-fronted Amazon (Amazona aestiva aestiva), *the nominate subspecies of the* aestiva *family.*

house cats are also very good hunters. In any case, one should never leave an amazon parrot kept at liberty unattended in the same room as a cat.

The way to an amazon parrot's heart is through its stomach

In the process of acclimating and taming, small treats given as a reward or as an occasional welcoming greeting sometimes work real miracles. Of course, it is not always true that the way to a man's heart is through his stomach, and not to an amazon parrot's either, but it often is. The amazon parrot should take the treat from the hand. Peanuts and almonds are well-suited for this purpose. It is important that the bird recognizes the treat as such; that is, that the same food is not present in its normal diet.

this may be that a dog, as a typical pack animal, considers all other creatures in its own home to be members of "its" pack. It can be more of a problem if the other pet is a cat. Like many other birds, amazon parrots often show an instinctive fear of cats. Also, not every cat is harmless for an amazon parrot; some out-and-out

With the amazon parrot in the outdoors

Fresh air and sunshine do all amazon parrots good. If it is not possible to keep the amazon parrot in the garden or on a balcony occasionally, then one can take it along on walks in the country. To avoid any potential mishaps, the amazon parrot should be chained by one foot. The most practical way to do this is with a removable ring together with a thin chain or a nylon or polyester cord. To avoid injury, foot rings for chaining should be made of rounded material.

An aviary allows a bird some illusion of freedom while providing him with a safe yet natural existence.

Trusting amazon parrots, which already know that there is a lot to discover and examine outside, will voluntarily lift a foot after a few excursions if they see you carrying the ring and cord. The chained amazon parrot is best carried perched on the forearm or the shoulder.

When the owner is not able to supervise the Amazon, it should always be kept in its cage.

Besides daily feeding, renewing of drinking water, and a few showers in the course of the week, amazon parrots do not require much care. It is far more important that one spends as much time with them as possible. How often one must thoroughly clean the cage depends on its size, but usually one cleaning a week is advisable. At least once a month one should brush off wire cages, perches, and so forth thoroughly with hot water.

A warm place?

Must amazon parrots, which after all come from an exotic climate, be kept particularly warm? No, because normally our room temperatures are

Facing: Yellow-fronted Amazon (Amazona ochrocephala). Claws must be kept to a short enough length for the bird to maintain healthy feet.

Nylabird™ products provide safe, healthy outlets for the Amazon's instinct to chew. These toys provide essential calcium, and they will help prevent the devastating habit of feather plucking. Nylabird™ products can be found in your local pet shop.

completely adequate for them. Nevertheless, it is advisable to keep newly imported birds at a somewhat a higher temperature at first. A new arrival should be treated carefully and protected from chilling and drafts. If one must air the room, a wool blanket should be placed over the cage. Once acclimated, most amazon parrot species are quite hardy. Birds that have already been acclimated to our climate over a number of years and are kept in outdoor aviaries can stay there until the onset of the first night frosts.

One should in any case be able to prepare a warm spot for one's amazon parrot in an emergency. As is true of almost all tropical birds, warmth is often the best medicine for "slight indisposition." A heat lamp is often helpful for this purpose, and one should have one available in case of need.

Claw and bill care

If the perches are of the correct diameter and the claws still grow too long, they must be clipped. A blood vessel, the "pulpa" is located in the middle of the claw. This should not be injured when cutting the claw. Clipping is done with claw clippers, such

Facing: *Blue-fronted Amazon* (Amazona aestiva).

as are used for trimming dogs' claws. If one has no experience in doing this, then one should have an expert demonstrate how to do it. It is an easy task with a really tame amazon parrot to clip a claw bit by bit while otherwise attending to the bird. It is simply a question of knowing how it is done. Should a claw ever happen to bleed, however, despite all caution, the bleeding can be stopped easily with the aid of cotton wool soaked with iron chloride.

If the upper mandible

Blue-fronted Amazon (Amazona aestiva). *The Amazon beak should be allowed to grow no longer than this. If necessary, have your veterinarian clip the bird's beak; do not attempt it yourself.*

grows too long or a bill correction of some other kind is necessary, which is extremely rare in amazon parrots, then one should definitely leave any operation to a veterinarian with a bird practice. In contrast to bleeding from injured claws, bleeding from injured bills can be extremely difficult to stop.

The plumage

If one has the opportunity to examine the plumage of a tame amazon parrot, then one will determine that its plumage contains feathers in all stages of development in addition to fully developed feathers. Amazon parrots, like all parrots, do not have a specific molting period. By molting is meant phases in which the majority or even the complete plumage is replaced within a short time. With amazon parrots, however, new feathers are grown and old ones are lost continuously. Only after breeding is it possible to observe a heavier feather change within a short time span in some amazon parrots.

With some amazon parrots,

Note how the Amazon's claws wrap around the perch. This action aids the wearing away of the claws.

Blue-fronted Amazon (Amazona aestiva) *on a store-bought perch.*

condition. Very rarely, individual Yellow-fronted Amazon Parrots are found with isolated blue feathers, and an individual Panama Amazon Parrot is known in which all of the normally green feathers were blue. To explain these occurrences, it must be pointed out that the two primary colors yellow and blue together form the color green. If the assimilation of the yellow or blue color component is disrupted for some reason during the development of the feather, then instead of green feathers, blue or yellow ones will result.

In order to make the plumage water-repellent, the feathers of parrots are continuously "powdered." The grayish white powder is produced by the powder down, which is abundantly distributed throughout the plumage. This powder gives the amazon parrot a somewhat "dusty" appearance, particularly if it has not bathed in a long time. Amazon parrots kept in the house should therefore have

one finds individual yellow feathers scattered throughout the ótherwise green plumage. If one of these yellow feathers falls out, then another yellow feather usually grows back in its place. It is only possible to speculate about the causes of this unusual coloration. These feathers are, however, by no means a sign of a deficiency or pathological

Facing: *Blue-fronted Amazon* (Amazona aestiva). *Amazons never bite out of maliciousness, only out of fear. This one is playing with its owner.*

Lilac-crowned Amazon (Amazona finschi) *on a natural perch.*

Clipping the wings

Amazon parrots that are kept at liberty in the house usually have their wings clipped, because keeping amazon parrots with full flying ability at liberty requires constant attention. When airing the house one must lock them up or chain them, and during the warm months screens must be installed over the windows. An amazon parrot kept at liberty with the complete run of the house produces quite a lot of dirt and can do much mischief. You should also never make the mistake of assuming that your amazon parrot is so tame and devoted that it would never fly away. Although a really tame amazon parrot that flies away is usually recovered, the runaway at the very least causes much concern and inconvenience.

It is often best to clip the amazon parrot's wings. It will also become accustomed to being near "its people" if its

an opportunity to shower often. This is most easily accomplished with a plant sprayer and lukewarm water. Once they have become used to it, amazon parrots will also shower under the bathroom shower or in the rain with relish.

Facing: *Blue-fronted Amazon* (Amazon aestiva). *Occasional bathing helps Amazon plumage remain fresh and clean looking.*

wings are clipped. An amazon parrot in full command of its flying abilities can of course easily evade any attempt to approach it. The wings of imported amazon parrots are usually clipped. If they are not, this should be done with newly acquired birds, with the exception of those birds that will be bred in aviaries. Even though flying ability varies between different species of amazon parrots, none of them can be considered good fliers, and some fly very poorly. For this reason, clipping a few feathers on each wing is often enough to hamper their flying. A simple clipping of the primaries is the easiest to do, but the clipped feathers are visible when the bird is perching. For this reason both wings should always be clipped, because birds with only one clipped wing could tumble over and hurt themselves during panicky attempts to fly. Because the clipped feathers will fall out after a while and will be replaced with new ones, the replacement feathers must also be clipped. This is easy to do with a tame amazon parrot: while playing with it, one clips the appropriate feathers little by little with short, sturdy clippers. One should not attempt to clip the wings of birds that are not tame; otherwise the parrot may associate this unpleasant experience with its provider. Parrot fanciers often help each other in this task, or it is left to an animal dealer. Clipping the wings of newly acquired birds protects against certain unpleasant surprises, and because the clipped feathers will grow back after a while, no permanent damage has been done. Later the amazon parrot can be kept at liberty or used for breeding.

A beautifully maintained Yellow-billed Amazon (Amazona collaria). A well cared for Amazon will have striking plumage, claws and bill which are in good shape, clear eyes, and an interested outlook on life.

Double Yellow-headed Amazon (Amazona ochrocephala oratrix), *and Panama Amazon* (Amazona ochrocephala panamensis). *These two subspecies are in great demand as pets.*

Idiosyncrasies and preferences

Even if their wings are not clipped, amazon parrots fly only reluctantly in confined areas; for example, in a small room. They prefer to reach their goal by walking and climbing. On level ground, they walk ceremoniously with a waddling gait, inward-turned feet, and a slightly raised tail. When climbing, they use their bill as a "grappling hook" or a "third leg."

The parrot holds large pieces of food with one foot and carries it to its bill to

Amazon parrots are amazingly supple and can use their feet to scratch areas that look impossible to reach.

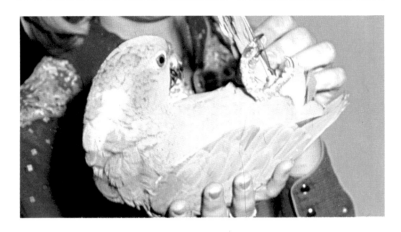

gnaw or bite off. It almost always uses the same foot for this, either the right or the left. Thus, among amazon parrots one finds definite right-handers and left-handers . . . I mean -footers!

All amazon parrots like to take showers. If kept outdoors, they enjoy rain showers with obvious relish. Amazon parrots kept indoors should therefore be showered with lukewarm

Yellow-naped Amazon (Amazona ochrocephala auropalliata). *Amazons can be trained to perform various tricks such as this.*

A stick trained Yellow-fronted Amazon (Amazona ochrocephala).

Blue-fronted Amazons (Amazona aestiva) enjoying a climbing session. Amazons love to climb on chains, but be sure that the chain is of a proper size to ensure the safety of the birds.

water several times a week. At first, one should use a water sprayer, such as is commonly used in the care of houseplants. Really tame amazon parrots can be taken into the bathroom and rinsed under the shower. Regular showering serves to make the plumage look well-groomed. Make sure that showers are given only at temperatures above about 18° C, so the bird does not catch cold.

Amazon parrots are by nature very gregarious birds. For this reason, amazon

Double Yellow-headed Amazon (Amazona ochrocephala oratrix) *taking a bath. Do not expose your Amazon to drafts at any time, especially after a bath when it is still wet.*

Facing: *Blue-fronted Amazon* (Amazona aestiva). *Amazons will climb anything vertical.*

Above: *Lilac-crowned Amazon* (Amazona finschi). *A tamed Amazon will quickly learn to ride on one's shoulder; it should not, however, be encouraged to ride on one's head.*

clearly shows a preference for women in its relations with people, this does not necessarily mean that it is a male.

Amazon parrots are monogamous. As long as an accident does not occur, they live with their mate over a long period of time, apparently even for life. For

Below: *Orange-winged Amazon* (Amazona amazonica). *Amazons are not afraid of heights.*

parrots kept singly, in particular, become strongly attached to the people in their environment. Not infrequently, the bird will give preference to a particular person or it will prefer either women or men. Contrary to a commonly held belief, this behavior has nothing to do with the amazon parrot's sex. Thus, if an amazon parrot

Double Yellow-headed Amazon (Amazona ochrocephala oratrix). Amazons love having their heads scratched.

Orange-winged Amazon (Amazona amazonica). *Singly kept Amazons will become devoted to their owner, but they are sometimes apt to be jealous of outsiders.*

this reason, it is not unusual for a singly kept amazon parrot to regard a particular person in its environment as its "mate." This behavior is especially common with birds that were either taken from their nest cavity or were captured immediately after leaving the nest and reared in captivity. Such birds, however, not only exhibit a strong attachment and unlimited trust in relation to

Blue-fronted Amazons (Amazona aestiva) are quick to attach themselves to their owners, but experts say they are also quick to exhibit jealousy.

their provider, they can also be aggressive toward other people while displaying all of the symptoms of jealousy. But by no means does every amazon parrot develop this kind of relationship with people, and often even completely tame birds, if they

Panama Amazon (Amazona ochrocephala panamensis). Screeching is a behavior which is worse in some species than in others, and it varies from bird to bird as well.

Yellow-naped Amazons (Amazona ochrocephala auropalliata) *are considered to be among the best Amazon talkers, and their voices are quite close to the human range.*

are given a choice, will prefer the company of other amazon parrots.

Talking amazon parrots

Many parrots have the ability to accurately imitate foreign sounds and noises, and this is also true of amazon parrots. Whether amazon parrots in the wild also mimic noises that are foreign to their species is disputed. It has often been claimed that amazon parrots do not do this in the wild, but detailed studies on this subject do not exist. I myself, however, once

Yellow-fronted Amazons (Amazona ochrocephala tresmariae). Two birds kept together will be less prone to boredom, but they will not learn to talk as easily as singly kept birds.

northwestern Brazil. This bird could accurately imitate the impudent scolding of capuchin monkeys. Unfortunately, it never divulged whether it had learned this noise while still in the rain forest or with a Brazilian animal collector or dealer.

Most amazon parrots kept as house pets learn to mimic sounds that they hear regularly after a while. But there is no way of knowing whether these sounds will include human speech, and if it does learn words, they will not necessarily be the exact words you wanted to teach the bird. I once had a humorous experience in this regard. A Blue-fronted

cared for a Festive Amazon Parrot many years ago during the quarantine period, which had come to us directly from

Double Yellow-headed Amazon (Amazona ochrocephala oratrix) on its back.

Yellow-fronted Amazon (Amazona ochrocephala).

Blue-fronted Amazon (Amazona aestiva) *in the act of preening itself.*

Amazon Parrot lived at liberty in the studio of an artist I knew. This amazon parrot was exceptionally small for its species and had unusual head markings. For this reason, I asked if I could photograph the bird. While I took out my camera and waited for a favorable moment to take a picture, he suddenly said to me loud and clear: "You're stupid!" It turned out that these were the only words that this amazon parrot had ever managed to learn. This is how it happened: in the beginning, its owner had wanted to teach it some polite manners and had pronounced for it clearly and often "good day,"

White-fronted Amazon (Amazona albifrons).

Above: *Mealy Amazon* (Amazona farinosa guatemalae).

greatly surprised when the bird greeted him one morning with "You're stupid." Disregarding its lack of talent for human speech, it never learned anything other than "You're stupid." This amazon parrot did have a good mimicking ability for other sounds, and could imitate the rattling of an alarm clock, the barking of a dog, and the meowing of a cat. It could also whistle short melodies fairly well. Not infrequently,

Below: *Mealy Amazon* (Amazona farinosa) *the nominative subspecies.*

"goodbye," "hello," "Pikusch is a fine bird." For months the amazon parrot had listened to all this patiently, but never said anything. Finally, the artist's patience was exhausted and he said, "You're stupid!" And subsequently he must also have said the same thing on more than one occasion. Some time later, he was

Vinaceous Amazon (Amazona vinacea), *one of the rarer Amazon breeds.*

Mealy Amazon (Amazona farinosa guatemalae).

then continues laughing again. It appears that laughing more closely resembles the internal "Amazonese" than other kinds of human sounds. In addition, amazon parrots most easily learn short words with at least two syllables, such as "Lora," "Anna," "Ida," and the like.

Once an amazon parrot starts to talk, it usually learns a few additional words, and a few can acquire a fairly large vocabulary. Amazon parrots, however, only rarely mimic human words with complete accuracy. They cannot compare with Grey Parrots with respect to exact acoustical reproduction. An amazon parrot also mimics only when it wants to; it never talks on command. It also tends to be silent in an unfamiliar environment. On one occasion, talking parrots were advertised in the local papers during a bird exhibition. To the disappointment of many visitors, not one parrot said anything during the first stage of the exhibition. After a week, a Grey Parrot finally began to talk, but all of the amazon parrots steadfastly remained silent. Then, on the last day of the exhibition, a visitor said, "I think that this thing with the talking amazon parrots is a fraud." He had

amazon parrots also learn to mimic human laughter in all its shades and pitches. In Sweden, a laughing Panama Amazon Parrot became known thoughout the country as the trademark of a nature program series. A Panama Amazon Parrot owned by friends of mine can also mimic peals of laughter. From time to time it interrupts itself to say "oh, how funny," and

Vinaceous Amazon (Amazona vinacea). Note the unusual beak coloration.

scarcely closed his mouth when an amazon parrot answered him with, "What did you say?" As stunning as the effect was on the bystanders, the amazon parrot of course did not know what it was saying. Its owner later told me that this "what did you say?" was actually one of the few word

Double Yellow-headed Amazon (Amazona ochrocephala oratrix).

combinations it had learned. On the other hand, talking amazon parrots do have the ability to react to and comment on a particular sequence of events or to specific sounds—so-called cues. If an amazon parrot regularly receives a bit of the breakfast egg in the morning, and each time the kitchen timer rings, which has been

Red-lored Amazons (Amazona autumnalis) are generally considered to be slow tamers.

Headstudy of a Mealy Amazon subspecies (Amazona farinosa chapmani).

for the talking ability of "his amazon parrot," because by no means do all amazon parrots learn to talk. In the overwhelming majority, the entire vocabulary consists of only a few precise words. Almost every amazon parrot will mimic, however; it is only a question of what. Some of them learn to mimic animal sounds or to whistle melodies. Others also imitate less pleasant sounds, such as squeaking doors or the sound of a vacuum cleaner.

"Are there differences between males and females with respect to mimicking ability?" and "are there differences between different species or subspecies in this respect?" are two frequently asked questions. The first question can be answered to the effect that there is no difference between the sexes with respect to mimicking ability. Some talking "Loras" have later been found to be males, and some talking "Jacobs" have later laid eggs. The second question is more difficult to answer objectively. I myself am familiar with two

used to time the eggs, one says, "Now here's your egg," then after a while it is quite possible that the bird will say "now here's your egg" whenever it hears the kitchen timer. It will, however, probably always repeat this phrase when it hears the timer, whether eggs are being cooked or not.

The owner of an amazon parrot is well advised not to have overly high expectations

Facing: *Hispaniolan Amazon* (Amazona ventralis).

amazon parrots that talk very well, of which one is a Panama Amazon Parrot and the other is a Yellow-naped Amazon Parrot, whereby the latter is even a true "talking genius." But others have also owned Blue-fronted Amazon Parrots, and so forth, that were good talkers. In my opinion, it would be a mistake to generalize these isolated observations and to consider this or that species to have greater talking ability. It is certain, however, that good talkers occur in all of the subspecies of *Amazona ochrocephala,* that is with the Yellow-fronted Amazon Parrot, Panama Amazon Parrot, Yellow-naped Amazon Parrot, and Double Yellow-fronted Amazon Parrot. One also finds good talkers among the Blue-fronted Amazon Parrot and Orange-winged Amazon Parrot. Of the more rarely imported species, there are without doubt also individuals of the Mealy Amazon Parrot with good mimicking ability. All Festive Amazon Parrots that I have been more closely acquainted with over the years quickly learned a few words, but then learned nothing else. At present, a pair of Festive Amazon Parrots live in the terrarium hall of the Skansen Aquarium in Stockholm where I work,

which, although they live together, talk readily and a lot, to the delight of visitors. After listening closely, it becomes evident that their entire vocabulary consists of only ten to twelve words. Very early in the morning one can hear a catalog of all of the sounds that can be heard in the place. Usually it is singly kept birds that develop their mimicking talent particularly well. Usually If several amazon parrots are kept together, they will speak only "Amazonese" amongst themselves.

Almost without exception, birds that have reached human hands at a very young age are the ones most likely to develop into good talkers. But what can an owner do to promote talking with his amazon parrot? A really gifted bird will, as long as it is not isolated from all sounds, begin talking on its own. Nevertheless, one can repeat the desired words several times a day loudly and well-articulated in front of the bird. A cassette recorder can make this task easier. Often, amazon parrots that doze completely relaxed in front of you are the most receptive. In any case, a lot of patience is required, and it can sometimes take months before the first attempt succeeds.

Double Yellow-headed Amazon (Amazona ochrocephala oratrix). *Amazons which are obtained when young will make better talkers than those birds obtained when nearing adulthood.*

Amazon parrots can be propagated very successfully in captivity. There are also good reasons to encourage breeding attempts of any kind with amazon parrots. Today the continued survival of many amazon parrot species in their natural living spaces is greatly endangered because of destruction of the environment. But obtaining species that are still common today by capturing them in the wild will probably also become more and more

Blue-fronted Amazon (Amazona aestiva).

difficult. Of course, the true animal lover will never consider catching the birds in the wild to be an ideal method of obtaining them. With many other parrots (for

Facing: *Yellow-fronted Amazon* (Amazona ochrocephala) *and Panama Amazon* (Amazona ochrocephala panamensis).

A trio of St. Lucia Amazons (Amazona versicolor). *These Amazons are rare and are not considered suitable as pets.*

example, with the many Australian parakeets or with African lovebirds), the demand is already largely met by birds bred in Europe. Why should something similar not be possible with amazon parrots?

For breeding attempts, aviary keeping is advantageous but by no means a requirement. I have had Blue-fronted Amazon Parrots that bred successfully in a wire cage with the dimensions of 120 by 60 by 100 centimeters. The fact that amazon parrot breeding has become increasing successful in recent years has two principal causes: first of all, today we know considerably more than before about amazon parrots, particularly how to feed them correctly. Second, today it is possible to make a definite sex determination in birds that will be used for breeding attempts. After all, the first requirement for a promising breeding attempt is a sure pair; that is, two birds that definitely include a male and a female. This would seem to be obvious, but is by no means a trivial consideration with amazon parrots. Apart from the White-fronted Amazon Parrot *(Amazona albifrons),* there are no differences in coloration between the sexes in amazon parrots. Moreover, two birds of the same species, if they have lived together for a long time, frequently behave exactly like a pair. If these are two females and one is really

Facing: *A breeding pair of Yellow-fronted Amazons* (Amazona ochrocephala ochrocephala).

A blue mutation of Panama Amazon (Amazona ochrocephala panamensis). *Mutations can occur in captivity as well as in the wild.*

characters is uncertain. A sure sex determination is possible by means of an endoscopic examination. In this procedure, the inside of the body of an anaesthesized bird is examined with the aid of a special instrument and it is determined whether ovaries or testicles are present. This procedure can, however, only be carried out on mature birds. At present, examinations of this kind are performed by only a few veterinarians. Nevertheless, one can often learn from the nearest veterinarian where sex determinations of this kind can be carried out. The expense of an examination of this kind may be money well spent. After all, there can be nothing more exasperating for a "breeder" than when he realizes that he has tried for years to breed two females or two males.

unlucky, they will even lay eggs and start incubating.

Sex determination
Generally, males differ from females in that they are more robust, their heads are somewhat larger, and the base of the bill is somewhat wider. These differences can, however, be more or less pronounced, and a sex determination based on these

Nest boxes and feeding
Although it is sometimes claimed that tame birds cannot be successfully bred, this is not true. This only applies to hand-reared amazon parrots that are

Facing: *Artist's rendering of a subspecies of Yellow-fronted Amazon* (Amazona ochrocephala tresmariae). *This subspecies is sometimes called the Tres Marias Double Yellow-headed Amazon.*

Yellow-fronted Amazon (Amazona ochrocephala) *poking its head out of a nest box.*

totally imprinted on human beings. Often, placid, confiding birds, which are not exactly finger tame, but which are not afraid of people, are the best suited.

In the wild, amazon parrots nest in natural tree cavities. If need be, they excavate the necessary nest cavity in rotting trees themselves with their powerful bills. For breeding in captivity, the inside of a hollow section of a linden, poplar, or willow trunk is often the best nesting facility as well. If a section of trunk of this kind cannot be obtained, then one can either build a nest box or have one built by a cabinet maker. In so doing, the following should be kept in mind: well-aged wood should be used,

Facing: *Orange-winged Amazon* (Amazona amazonica) *and Red-lored Amazon* (Amazona autumnalis).

because nest boxes of freshly sawed wood often are not entered for months. The boards that are used should be at least 2.5 centimeters thick. Unplaned boards, or those that have been planed on one side only with the unplaned side to the inside, should be used. The interior dimensions of the nest box should be 25 by 25 by 40 centimeters. For the largest species the size can be increased to 30 by 30 by 50 centimeters. The entrance hole, which should be located in the upper third of the front

White-fronted Amazons (Amazona albifrons) *inside a twelve by twelve by twenty-four inch nest box.*

Yellow-naped Amazon (Amazona ochrocephala auropalliata).

wall, should have a diameter of ten to twelve centimeters. A piece of branch attached under the entrance hole is recommended to make landing easier. All nest boxes should be provided with an inspection hole located just above the floor.

Amazon parrots do not use nesting material; the bottom of the nest box is simply

Double Yellow-headed Amazon (Amazona ochrocephala oratrix).

covered with a layer of wood shavings. Before putting the nest box into service it should be soaked in water for at least a day so that the wood absorbs as much moisture as possible. The reason for this is that relatively high humidity is necessary for the normal development of the embryo in the egg. About 70 percent humidity is required for amazon parrots. In outdoor nest boxes this is almost always ensured, assuming that the nest box is hung up in such a way that it is not exposed to direct sunlight. Inside buildings with central heating, on the other hand, one should use a humidifier

Yellow-fronted Amazon (Amazona ochrocephala ochrocephala).

Facing: *St. Lucia Amazon* (Amazona versicolor).

White-fronted Amazons (Amazona albifrons) *at two weeks, top, and four weeks, bottom.*

during breeding attempts in winter. Because incubating amazon parrots can also carry moisture into the nest box, they should be showered with a sprayer when the opportunity arises during the incubation period.

Diet is the key to successful breeding. First of all, the percentage of protein in the diet should be increased in breeding attempts. In so doing one must determine by trial and error what the birds like to eat. I feed my birds dry dog food and cooked egg as "protein supplements." Some amazon parrots also like to eat cooked fish. The "breeding pellets" for parrots, which have recently appeared on the market, are also very high in protein. In addition to these protein-rich foodstuffs, sprouted seeds also have a positive effect on the breeding drive. Large amounts of fruit and greens should also be provided. Soaked zwieback, to which one adds a few drops of a multivitamin supplement, rounds out the menu.

Breeding and rearing

Amazon parrots generally breed during our spring months, but birds that have been kept inside for some time may also breed at other times of the year. During the courtship display, males, in particular, can be observed running back and forth on a perch with spread tail and ruffled nape feathers, while emitting screechy calls and contracting their pupils. For the actual mating act, the male climbs on the female's back from the side, where it holds tight with the feet and bill. Mating lasts several minutes in amazon parrots, during which time the male presses its cloaca against that of the female.

As a rule, two to four eggs

are laid at intervals of two to three days. The female start incubating as soon as the first egg is laid. The incubation period lasts 28 to 30 days, and during this time the female is fed primarily by the male, because incubating females usually leave the nest box only for short periods of time. One should keep in mind that amazon parrots are very aggressive during this time, which is especially true of otherwise tame birds. Cleaning the cage, or even an aviary, is usually out of the question; one should simply let the dirt pile up. It is better not to disturb the breeding pair.

Young amazon parrots have a long period of development, and it takes 60 to 70 days before they are able to leave the nest cavity.

Yellow-fronted Amazon (Amazona ochrocephala) *at nineteen days.*

During this time they are fed from their parents' crop: first by the female alone and later by both parents. Some youngsters return to the nest at night even after they have left the nest, whereas others spend the night outside the box from the start. The youngsters now gradually begin to feed on their own. At this stage they prefer soft food. Nevertheless, they continue to be fed by the parents, now primarily by the male, and only when they have reached four months in

Blue-fronted Amazons (Amazona aestiva) *in a breeding cage.*

Double Yellow-headed Amazon (Amazona ochrocephala oratrix) *at nine weeks.*

age do they feed completely independently.

An important question should still be answered: at what age are breeding attempts promising with amazon parrots? As far as it is known, there is only a single account of an amazon parrot that is supposed to have bred in its second year. This is, however, certainly an exception. Almost all birds that have bred successfully were at least four years old. We are not yet sure what the upper limit is, but amazon parrots are apparently capable of reproduction up to an age of 30 years, if not longer. One of our female Blue-fronted Amazon Parrots bred successfully for the first time after it had lived with us in the zoo for a documented 23 years. Therefore, it could well have been more than 25 years old when it reared its first youngster.

General health care

The first symptoms of illness

Once properly acclimated and adjusted to our climate, amazon parrots are quite hardy and resistant charges. But they too can of course become ill. Because of their high metabolisms, illnesses in birds often take a considerably more rapid course than in mammals. Therefore, it is particularly important with them to ascertain the onset of an illness as early as possible. An incipient illness can usually be recognized in that the amazon parrot does not behave as usual. A good awareness of its "normal" behavior thus also makes it easier to recognize the first symptoms of an illness.

As the owner of an amazon parrot, one should also know

A healthy bird has eyes which are free of discharge, as does this Yellow-fronted Amazon (Amazona ochrocephala).

where one can obtain veterinary advice and assistance in the event of an illness. One cannot simply expect to visit the best possible veterinarian with a sick amazon parrot already on one's hands. By no means all veterinarians are trained to treat sick birds. Usually one can learn from the veterinarian where one can find the nearest bird specialist. But

A Blue-fronted Amazon (Amazona aestiva) *with a healthy appetite.*

because illnesses in birds run their course very rapidly, valuable time will be lost in an emergency before one finds the right veterinarian. It is better to obtain the information ahead of time.

Feathers from a Double Yellow-headed Amazon (Amazona ochrocephala oratrix).

Conditions that promote the outbreak of illnesses and not infrequently also precede the appearance of infectious diseases are rapid cooling, draft, stress, and unsuitable diet. Illnesses associated with shipping or sudden changes are therefore not rare. Typical indications that something is not right with an amazon parrot are lack of appetite; ruffled, fluffed plumage; weakness; and sleeping on both feet or even on the bottom of the cage. Just as abnormal are a swollen crop; diarrhea; persistent sneezing;

Facing: *Imperial Amazon* (Amazona imperialis).

discharge from the nostrils; ragged breathing, whereby the tail moves up and down with each breath; encrusted or swollen eyelids; and disturbances of equilibrium. These symptoms can show up singly or several can appear simultaneously.

A clear-eyed Yellow-billed Amazon (Amazona collaria).

Prevention and healing
The first step in any illness consists of keeping the bird warm and out of drafts. To this end one uses a heat lamp, which is installed over the bird in such a way that a temperature of 35 to 40° C is maintained in its environment. The bird must be able to retreat from the direct rays of the lamp at any time.

If the bird has eaten spoiled food, a crop obstruction can result. The crop consists of a bipartite, sac-like dilation of the esophagus. Its function is the predigestion of food, and after a while the food passes from it to the proventriculus and then to the ventriculus. When food is eaten, the left

A beautiful ten year old Yellow-fronted Amazon (Amazona ochrocephala ochrocephala). Preening is essential to a bird's health and sanity.

half of the crop is always filled first, which can often be recognized by a slight swelling of the left side of the neck.

If the crop swells greatly and persistently, a crop obstruction could be present.

Pair of White-fronted Amazons (Amazona albifrons).

For treatment, the bird should first go without food for 24 hours and then should be given cooked rice to which a little lemon juice has been added. If the swelling does not go down, a veterinarian must be called in. In an emergency, a crop obstruction can be surgically treated.

Diarrhea caused by changes in diet or stress can usually be cleared up quickly with a diet of cooked rice.

If a diet of cooked rice does not bring about the desired result with diarrhea, one should again consult the veterinarian, because an intestinal infection caused by coli, coccid, or salmonella bacteria could be present. These illnesses hardly ever occur with birds kept indoors. In outdoor aviaries, on the other hand, these illnesses can be transmitted by other animals (for example, crows, sparrows, pigeons, mice, and the like). An unnatural concentration of coccid bacteria on the floor of the

Green-cheeked Amazon (Amazona viridigenalis).

Green-cheeked Amazons (Amazona viridigenalis) *at liberty together. Amazons that are given complete outdoor freedom are at risk to catch many avian diseases from wild birds.*

aviary is not unusual under poor hygienic conditions. Treatment takes place with antibiotics or sulfa drugs under a veterinarian's supervision.

Symptoms of sneezing and moist nostrils in an amazon parrot are usually the result of a chill; for example, caused by draft. These symptoms are characteristic of an illness that we usually call a "cold." If these symptoms have persisted for a long time or are accompanied by eye inflammation or by slimy

Red-lored Amazon (Amazona autumnalis).

yellow-green diarrhea, one should definitely call in a veterinarian. It could namely be a question of parrot fever (ornithosis). Every parrot owner, and anyone who keeps any kind of bird, should be acquainted with this illness in his own and in his birds' interest. This disease is caused by a microorganism, which today is classified with the bacteria under the name Chlamydia ornithosis. Because it occupies an intermediate position between the bacteria and viruses, it was previously known by the names Miyagawanella or Bedsonia. In this disease there is no typical course of illness. All symptoms from a slight cold up to serious attacks on the respiratory and digestive organs are possible. An infection can result just as easily through dusty, dried droppings as through droplets released in sneezing. A sure diagnosis is only possible by means of a serological blood test. Since a test of this kind takes a long time, a veterinarian will already begin treatment with specific antibiotics (tetracycline) on the basis of a justifiable suspicion. It is important to know that birds that appear to be healthy can also be carriers of this disease, and that the

obligatory preventive treatment of all parrots during quarantine does not rule out the illness with one hundred percent certainty. Timely and proper treatment will allow birds to survive in most cases. With birds that refuse to eat because of the illness, the appropriate antibiotics can be injected.

Basic knowledge about this illness is important because ornithosis can be transmitted to human beings. Every bird fancier should always alert the treating physician to the possibility of an ornithosis infection if he has an illness of the respiratory tract. This illness is by no means restricted to parrots—despite the name "parrot fever"— but, on the contrary, can also infect many other kinds of birds. With people, the illness is also treated with tetracycline. Choosing the right antibiotic is extremely important, because some antibiotics, such as penicillin, have no effect.

Another insidious illness that can attack the respiratory tract and air sacs of amazon parrots is aspergillosis. This illness is caused by fungi of the genus Aspergillus, the spores of which are inhaled by the bird. Because this fungus is present almost everywhere, the danger of an infection

although the treatment is relatively expensive. The medicine available for treatment, Daktarin (Janssen), must be injected into the muscles daily over a fairly long period of time. The dosage for amazon parrots is 0.5 ml daily over a period of at least 20 days, possibly longer.

Vitamin deficiency illnesses need scarcely be feared with an all-around diet. Should disturbances in equilibrium nevertheless appear with amazon parrots, the affected birds must immediately be

Red-crowned Amazon (Amazona dufresniana rhodocorytha).

Yellow-shouldered Amazon (Amazona barbadendis).

exists with birds that are otherwise weakened. With amazon parrots, the illness almost exclusively strikes newly imported birds that are in poor condition. In contrast, this illness rarely affects acclimated birds.
Aspergillosis must always be suspected if treatment with antibiotics is unsuccessful in an infection of the respiratory organs. In contrast to the past, aspergillosis can be effectively treated today,

Blue-fronted Amazon (Amazona aestiva).

given large doses of the entire vitamin B complex. Disturbances in equilibrium can naturally also have other cause; for example, cerebral hemorrhages or epilepsy in very old birds. A sudden vitamin B deficiency in normal seeds because of poor storage conditions can, however, never be completely ruled out with disturbances in equilibrium, and therefore one should not hesitate to administer vitamin B immediately in these cases. If the cause was something else, then no harm was done.

Parasitic infestation by intestinal parasites in the form of tapeworms (Cestodes) can occur in newly imported birds. Tapeworms reveal their presence through the pieces of broken white segments one finds in the droppings. Threadworm and roundworm infestations can also occur in amazon parrots. Whereas roundworms are strictly host-specific in parrots (that is, parrots have their "own" kinds of roundworms), threadworms can also be transmitted by other birds (for example, in an outdoor aviary). If a worm infestation is suspected, the first step is to send a sample of the droppings to a veterinary laboratory, the address of which can be obtained from the nearest veterinarian. If an examination of the sample shows that a worm infestation is present, a worming treatment will be carried out under the supervision of a veterinarian. The worming cure consists of a series of treatments in which the prescribed time intervals must be followed exactly; otherwise the cure may not be successful. It should also be noted that an infection of human beings with these avian parasites need not be feared.

Skin and feather parasites

such as bird mites or feather lice (Mallophaga) are extremely rare with amazon parrots, which in part can certainly be attributed to their intensive grooming. In the event one does find skin or feather parasites on one's amazon parrots, one should never use an insecticide powder or spray, but instead ask a veterinarian for advice.

Fairly small wounds should only be sprinkled with an antibiotic powder. Minor injuries heal rapidly in amazon parrots. If an amazon parrot should, however, happen to receive a more serious wound or even a broken bone, as the result of an accident, for example, then the treatment definitely should be left to a veterinarian.

Medications that the bird is supposed to eat can often be mixed with its favorite food. If the bird will not take the medicine in liquid form from a small spoon, then one should use a one-way syringe (without the hypodermic

A pair of young Yellow-fronted Amazons (Amazona ochrocephala).

needle). If the bird must be held while administering medications, it must never be turned on its back. If you must hold your amazon parrot for the treatment, it is often easier to wrap it in a blanket and pull out the part of the body, such as a foot or a wing, that requires treatment than to use heavy gloves. Really frightened amazon parrots can even bite through thick gloves hard enough to leave bruises.

Finally, a few words about feather eating and feather plucking. This phenomena is far rarer in amazon parrots than in Grey Parrots and macaws. Feather eating and feather plucking are not illnesses in the true sense of the word, even though itchy skin caused by an infestation of feather lice may possibly contribute to its occurrence. If parrots systematically pull out or bite off feathers, psychological causes are generally responsible. This phenomenon is almost unknown with amazon parrots that are kept with other parrots. With birds kept singly, the prolonged absence of the provider can sometimes be the triggering factor. No promising treatment with the aid of medications is known. Nevertheless, it is not unusual for feather eaters to

give up their "vice" when their living conditions are drastically altered. If possible, companionship of its own kind is still the most promising solution.

For the reader who wants to learn more about bird diseases and their treatment, a listing of specialized literature can be found at the end of this book.

Dangers in house and garden

If one occasionally lets an amazon parrot out of the cage or if one keeps it at liberty in the house at all times, then to what dangers will the feathered housemate thereby be exposed? In the first place, substances that can be dangerous to people (small children, in particular) as well as house pets should be mentioned. Such things as caustic solutions, solvents, detergents, insecticides, and the like must not be left standing around.

Another source of danger, to which some parrots have fallen victim, is poisonous house plants. Among our most popular house plants there are some that are poisonous. Because people do not consider these plants to be "vegetables," they do not normally pose a danger to us. But an amazon parrot at liberty will of course taste all the greens it can reach. Particularly poisonous are the oleander (Nerium oleander), nux vomica (Strychnos nux-vomica), and lesser periwinkle (Vinca minor).

Yellow-shouldered Amazon (Amazona barbadendis rothschildi). *This subspecies is sometimes called Rothschild's Amazon.*

Care is also advised with all species of the genus Dieffenbachia, the leaves of which are highly poisonous for parrots. If an amazon parrot is also allowed in the garden, one should keep in mind that even among our most common ornamental plants there are some that are poisonous. These include the clematis, all acacia

shrubs (Robinia), and yews (Taxus).

Furthermore, a warning against bitter almonds is also in order, because cases of parrot poisonings by bitter almonds are known. Bitter almonds, which are used as an aromatic ingredient in the making of marzipan, contain

A preening Double Yellow-headed Amazon (Amazona ochrocephala oratrix).

152

hydrocyanic acid. Bitter almonds can be distinguished from sweet almonds not only by their bitter taste, but because they are only about half as large as sweet almonds.

An amazon parrot owner wouldn't intentionally give his charge spoiled food. Fungus can appear in improperly stored seeds, however, which, at least in some cases, produce highly toxic substances. It is not always easy to see a fungal infestation of this kind, but it usually reveals itself by its moldy smell. One should always be attentive when buying seeds, and preferably stick one's nose in the bag.

Open electrical wiring in

Be sure to keep household plants away from your birds. Many common plants are lethal to Amazons.

Red-necked Amazon (Amazona arausiaca).

touch both poles with its dry tongue is slight. More serious in this regard is the danger that the damaged electrical cord itself will become a source of danger because of the possibility of fire. Amazon parrots, like all birds, are highly sensitive to the vapors of solvents of all kinds. Before any painting or any other repairs in which paint, varnish, glue, and the like, as well as the solvents used with them, such as turpentine, paint thinner, trichloroethylene, and acetone are used, amazon parrots should be removed from the rooms in question.

Nevertheless, because conditions are different in every house and apartment, I recommend that you logically consider what other sources of danger could be present.

the house can be a source of danger. Many a cable or electrical cord has been gnawed through by amazon parrots. Only rarely does an adventure of this kind result in injury to the amazon parrot. The horn of its bill, after all, does not conduct electricity, and the likelihood that it will simultaneously

Facing: *St. Vincent Amazon* (Amazona guildingii).

The following books by T.F.H. Publications are available in your local pet shop.

HANDBOOK OF AMAZON PARROTS
By Dr. A. E. Decoteau
ISBN 0-87666-892-9
TFH H-1025

Contents: The Amazon Parrots. Housing Amazon Parrots. Feeding the Amazons. Amazons in Exhibitions. Breeding the Amazons. The Endangered Amazons. Preventive Medicine. Common Ailments and Diseases Affecting Amazons. Pacheco's Disease—The Great Parrot Danger. The Species of Amazon Parrots (Fifty-six species and subspecies discussed).
Audience: This book is of great value to anyone who owns or contemplates owning an Amazon parrot. All important aspects of caring for and housing and feeding the birds is covered (there is even a chapter on *breeding* Amazon parrots, coverage of value to even the most advanced fanciers). In addition, the author manages to convey to the reader the subtle but important differences in personality and talking ability among the different Amazons. The many full-color photos in this book serve as excellent guides to identification of the species and subspecies. Suitable for readers of all ages.
Hard cover, 5½ x 8', 256 pages. Illustrated with 80 full-color photos, 51 black and white photos, 41 line drawings.

THE WORLD OF AMAZON PARROTS
By Dieter Hoppe
ISBN 0-86622-928-0
TFH H-1093

Contents: Behavior in the Wild. Amazons in Captivity. Breeding. The CITES Treaty. The Species. Bibliography. Indexes.
Audience: All of the Amazon parrots are included here, with comments on each of the subspecies. Besides the sections treating these birds as a group, each species has details particular to it treated separately. General care, accommodations, purchase, keeping, taming, diet, and illness are the main categories of the discussion, which seeks to clarify the relation between the natural habits of the birds and their needs in captivity.
Hard cover, contains many full-color photos.

YELLOW-FRONTED AMAZON PARROTS
By Dr. Edward J. Mulawka
ISBN 8-87666-835-X
T.F.H. PS-781

Contents: Introduction. General Characteristics of *Amazona ochrocephala.* Breeding Amazon Parrots. The Subspecies of Amazona ochrocephala.

Hard cover 5½ x 8', 128 pages; Illustrated with over 30 full-color photos and numerous black and white photos

Index

AMAZON PARROTS
TS-115